CHANGING WORLD

RUSSIA

CHANGING WORLD

RUSSIA

Simon Adams

ARCTURUS

This edition first published in 2010 by Arcturus Publishing
Distributed by Black Rabbit Books
P.O. Box 3263
Mankato
Minnesota MN 56002

Printed in China

Library of Congress Cataloging-in-Publication Data

Adams, Simon, 1955-
  Russia / Simon Adams.
      p. cm. -- (Changing world)
  Includes index.
  ISBN 978-1-84837-645-8 (library bound)
  1. Russia (Federation)--Juvenile literature. 1. Title.

  DK510.23.A33 2011
  947.086--dc22

                         2009051188

Series concept: Alex Woolf
Editor and picture researcher: Jacqueline McCann
Designer: Ian Winton
Maps and charts: Stefan Chabluk

Picture credits:
Corbis: cover right (Sergei Ilnitsky), 16 (Bettman Standard RM), 17 (Historical Standard RM),
18 (Michael Samojeden), 20 (Alexander Natruskin), 21 (Ivan Vdovin/JAI), 22 (Swim Ink 2, LLC),
24 top (EPA), 24 bottom (Peter Endig/dpa), 27 (Yuri Kochetkov/EPA), 31 (Sergei Chirikov/EPA),
32 (Dmitri Baltermants), 34 (Yuri Kochetkov/EPA), 36 (Gerd Ludwig), 42 (Yuri Kotchetkov/EPA).
Getty: 3 & 9 (Charley Yelen), 6 (Dean Conger), 8 (Arctic-Images), 10 (AFP/Stringer), 11 (Bruno Morandi),
12 (Time Life Pictures), 13 (Victor Mikhailovich Vasnetsov), 14 (Tim Graham), 15 (Hulton Archive/Stringer),
23 (Yuri Kadobnov/AFP), 25 (AFP/Stringer), 28 (Demetrio Carrasco), 29 (Alexey Sazonov/Stringer),
37 (Doug Allan), 39 (Louisa Gouliamaki/ Stringer), 40 (Oleg Nikishin), 41 (Dimitar Dilkoff), 43 (Epsilon).
Flickr: 17 (Denis Sarkic), 19 (World Economic Forum/Remy Steinegger), 38 (Mitya Aleshkovsky).
NHPA cover left (Bryan and Cherry Alexander).
Science Photo Library: 35 (Ria Novosti).
Shutterstock: 26 (Denis Babenko).

Cover captions
Left: Nenet woman from Yamal, northwest Siberia.
Right: Gazprom logo highlighted in front of Russian government building.

ISBN: 978-1-84837-645-8
SL001315US
Supplier 03, Date 0210

Contents

CHAPTER 1

Introduction

The Russian Federation, usually known just as Russia, is by far the largest country in the world. It is almost twice as big as China and extends halfway around the globe. It sprawls across eastern Europe and all of northern Asia, covering 11 different time zones. Russia

Much of northern Russia, including Siberia, is covered with vast coniferous forest that stretches for thousands of miles. This empty region is drained by large rivers that flow north into the Arctic Ocean.

lies between the Baltic Sea in the west, the Pacific Ocean in the east, the Arctic Ocean in the north, and the Caspian and Black seas in the south. The Bering Strait at the eastern tip of Russia separates Russia from North America and the state of Alaska. Fourteen other countries border Russia; only China has as many neighbors.

European Russia

The western, or European, part of Russia (28 percent of the total country) lies at the eastern end of the vast, low-lying North European Plain. This plain stretches from the North Sea east across Germany, Poland, Belarus, and Russia to the Ural Mountains. In Russia, this fertile area is drained by the Volga, Don, and other large, south-flowing rivers. In the far south, the Caucasus Mountains, containing Mount Elbrus

PHYSICAL GEOGRAPHY

Total area: 6,659,328 square miles (17,075,200 square kilometers, sq km)

Highest point: Mount Elbrus, 18,506 feet (5,642 meters, m)

Lowest point: Volga Delta, Caspian Sea: 92 feet (28 m) below sea level

Coastline: 23,345 miles (37,653 km)

Major rivers: Ob', Irtysh, Amur, Volga, Yenisey, Lena

Major cities: Moscow, St. Petersburg, Novosibirsk, Nizhniy Novgorod, Yekaterinburg, Samara, Omsk

Source: CIA *World Factbook*

The map contains the following labels:

ATLANTIC OCEAN

IRELAND

UNITED KINGDOM

NETHERLANDS

NORWAY

DENMARK

GERMANY

SWEDEN

FINLAND

Baltic Sea

Kaliningrad (RUSSIA)

ESTONIA

LITHUANIA

LATVIA

Lake Ladoga

Neva River

White Sea

Murmansk

ARCTIC OCEAN

Barents Sea

Kara Sea

Laptev Sea

East Siberian Sea

Bering Strait

Alaska (US)

Bering Sea

Anadyr River

Penzhina River

PACIFIC OCEAN

KAMATCHKA PENINSULA

Sea of Okhotsk

Kolyma River

Lena River

Arctic Circle

CZECH REPUBLIC

POLAND

SLOVAKIA

HUNGARY

BELARUS

Minsk

Smolensk

St. Petersburg

Novgorod

Lake Onega

Key
○ Cities over 1 million people
● Cities under 1 million people
△ Mountain
-·-· Trans-Siberian Railway
～ Border of former USSR

CENTRAL SIBERIAN UPLANDS

WEST SIBERIAN PLAIN

URAL MOUNTAINS

RUSSIAN FEDERATION

Moscow (capital)

ROMANIA

UKRAINE

MOLDOVA

BULGARIA

Sea of Azov

Black Sea

Rostov-na-Donu

Nizhniy Novgorod

Kazan

Ufa

Samara

Volga River

Yekaterinburg

Chelyabinsk

Ob' River

Yenisey River

Omsk

Irtysh River

Novosibirsk

Lake Baikal

Amur River

CHINA

JAPAN

Vladivostok

Sea of Japan

NORTH KOREA

SOUTH KOREA

Kuban River

Sochi

Mount Elbrus △

Chechnya

Groznyy

CAUCASUS MOUNTAINS

GEORGIA

TURKEY

ARMENIA

AZERBAIJAN

Caspian Sea

Volgograd

KAZAKHSTAN

Aral Sea

UZBEKISTAN

SYRIA

IRAQ

IRAN

TURKMENISTAN

KYRGYZSTAN

TAJIKISTAN

AFGHANISTAN

MONGOLIA

CHINA

N

0 miles 1,000
0 kilometers 1,000

(Russia's and Europe's highest mountain), run between the Black and Caspian seas. They form the border between Europe and Asia. The port of Murmansk on the Barents Sea and ports on the Black Sea and Sea of Azov are the only all-weather ports in Russia. Those on the Baltic, Arctic, and Pacific coastlines are frozen solid in winter.

Asian Russia

The Ural Mountains form the eastern border of Europe with Asia. Beyond them lies Asian Russia. This vast region, known as Siberia, comprises 72 percent of Russia and is bigger than the US and Western Europe combined. Northern Siberia lies along the shores of the Arctic Ocean and is mostly within the Arctic Circle. This cold region consists of a treeless plain known as the tundra.

Russia spreads across the continents of Asia and Europe. The tiny enclave of Kaliningrad, in the far west of the country, is separated from the rest of Russia by Belarus, Latvia, and Lithuania.

Its subsoil remains frozen all year round while its surface melts during the summer months to form a boggy, mosquito-ridden marsh. Farther south, the rest of Siberia is covered by a huge coniferous forest. Many large rivers, notably the Ob', Yenisey, and Lena, drain north into the Arctic Ocean. Lake Baikal, close to the southern border with Mongolia, is, at 5,370 feet (1,637 m) deep, the deepest lake in the world. Its vast size holds one-fifth of the world's freshwater. The far east of the region, bordering the Pacific Ocean, is mountainous and remote.

Anadyr, a mining town in the Chukotka region of northeast Siberia, is one of the coldest cities in Russia. It has an extremely harsh climate: in January, the temperature dips from −4°F (−20°C) to −49°F (−45°C). In July, it never rises above 50°F (10°C).

Climate

Russia has a cold, continental climate that produces two very different main seasons. The almost uniformly freezing winters vary little from north to south but are far more extreme in the east. This is because the country is exposed to cold weather from the Arctic Ocean to its north but shielded by the Himalayas and other mountain ranges to its south and east. These prevent the warm, moist winds of the Indian and Pacific oceans from reaching the country. A temperature of −94 degrees Fahrenheit, °F (−70 degrees Celcius, °C) recorded in February 1892 at Verkhoyansk in Siberia is the lowest temperature ever recorded outside Antarctica.

The temperature in Moscow is at, or well below, freezing for five months of the year, with a short spring and autumn. The three summer months are warm. Rainfall is low throughout the year, peaking in mid-summer.

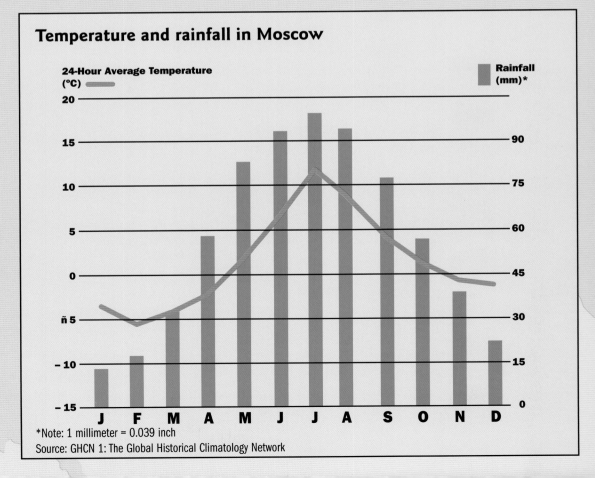

Temperature and rainfall in Moscow

24-Hour Average Temperature (°C)

Rainfall (mm)*

*Note: 1 millimeter = 0.039 inch

Source: GHCN 1: The Global Historical Climatology Network

Land use

European Russia is rich in minerals and raw materials, including oil, coal, and iron ore. The land is heavily farmed, particularly in the fertile, black soils of the steppes that stretch from the border with Ukraine in the east to beyond Novosibirsk in southern Siberia. This region supports cattle, pigs, and sheep. Cereals, particularly wheat, and crops for industrial use are all grown, as are root crops such as potatoes and sugar beet, which provide fodder for animals. The south is warm enough to grow rice, sunflowers, citrus fruits, grapes, and tobacco.

Northern Russia and most of Siberia are heavily wooded and support forestry, fishing, reindeer herding, and wild animal hunting. Vegetables are grown in hothouses in the urban areas. Like European Russia, Siberia is rich in minerals and raw materials, including gold, diamonds, oil, and natural gas.

The main industrial areas in Russia are in the Volga river valley, the Urals, the northwestern Kola peninsula, and southern Siberia. Lighter manufacturing industries are concentrated in the urban areas of western Russia. Isolated mining towns are scattered throughout all of Siberia and the Arctic regions.

The Altai Mountains straddle the border between Russian Siberia, China, Mongolia, and Kazakhstan. This area, a UNESCO World Heritage Site, is under pressure from people who live there to develop economically.

The Russian people

The 2002 census recorded 145,166,731 people living in Russia. Four-fifths are ethnic Russians, with the remaining one-fifth representing 160 different Slav and non-Slav ethnic groups. Russia's population density is only 3 people per square mile (8 people per sq km) because the country is so big. By comparison, the population density of the US is 12 people per square mile (32 people per sq km). The official language is Russian, and it is written in the Cyrillic alphabet. Many of the different nationalities speak their own officially recognized local languages, which they write in their own alphabet or in the Latin alphabet used to write English and other European languages.

From 1922–91, Russia was one of 15 republics inside the USSR, or Soviet Union. When the union collapsed, many Russians found themselves living in what to them were foreign countries. They formed about one-third of the population in each of the republics of Kazakhstan, Estonia, and Latvia. Similarly, many Ukrainians, Armenians,

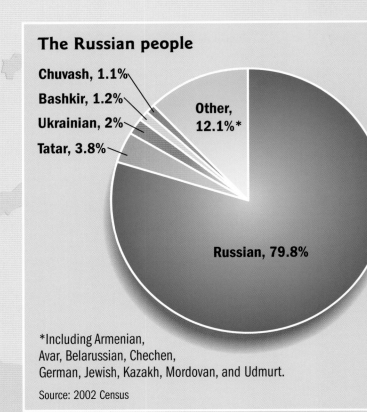

The Russian people

Chuvash, 1.1%
Bashkir, 1.2%
Ukrainian, 2%
Tatar, 3.8%
Other, 12.1%*
Russian, 79.8%

*Including Armenian, Avar, Belarussian, Chechen, German, Jewish, Kazakh, Mordovan, and Udmurt.

Source: 2002 Census

Four out of every five people who live in the Russian Federation are ethnic Russians. The remaining one-fifth is drawn from 160 different ethnic groups, some numbering no more than 10,000 people.

Kazakhs, and others found themselves in Russia. Some of the former Soviet republics, such as

These Russian women from a village near St. Petersburg celebrate the traditional festival of Shrovetide to mark the end of winter and the beginning of the Christian festival of Lent. They are dressed traditionally and compete to knock each other off the beam.

The Trans-Siberian Railway starts in Moscow and ends in Vladivostok on the Pacific coastline. Train passengers travel through seven time zones and spend more than six days on board. Construction of the railroad began in 1891 and was completed in 1916.

Kyrgyzstan, tried to keep their Russian population because they needed its skills. Most, however, discriminated against Russian minorities, forcing them to meet local language and residency requirements to gain citizenship. As a result, many Russians left the former republics and emigrated to Russia itself.

Urban and rural

Seventy-three percent of the Russian population lives in cities, the rest in the countryside. The capital, Moscow, is home to 10.13 million people. St. Petersburg, formerly known as Leningrad, has a population of 4.16 million, while five other cities all have populations over 1 million. The Russian population is not evenly spread across the country, with around 100 million people living in European Russia and only 40 million in Siberia.

Transportation

The quickest way to travel in Russia is by air since distances between the major cities are vast. The main carrier, Aeroflot International Russian

Airlines, competes with three other, smaller international airlines. A series of regional "babyflot" airlines fly domestic routes. The high-speed Sokol ("falcon") rail link connects St. Petersburg to Moscow while the world-famous Trans-Siberian Railway connects Moscow with Vladivostok, 5,759 miles (9,288 km) and six days, four hours away to the east. Moscow has an excellent metro system, and other cities are served by streetcar, trolleybus, and bus services. In rural areas, car ownership is low and people rely more on efficient bus networks.

Changing Russia

Modern Russia is changing rapidly. It only emerged as an independent nation in 1991 and has since undergone a massive political, social, and economic revolution that has affected every aspect of people's lives. Russia was once part of a major world empire and is now struggling to find a new role. Its people are facing a very different world from the one lived in by their parents and grandparents.

CHAPTER 2

History

The history of Russia begins in 862 CE, when the Slav peoples of Novgorod, a city in northwest modern Russia, invited Rurik—a Varangian, or Viking, originally from Scandinavia—to rule over them. It is probable that the Viking Varangians, rather than the Slavs of Novgorod, were the original Rus, but the new rulers soon married into the local Slav population and adopted their language and customs.

Kiev and Christianity

Twenty years later, the Varangian prince Oleg of Novgorod occupied Kiev—now capital of Ukraine—and made it the first capital of the Rus. At this time, the Rus lived in a long strip of land in what is now Russia, Belarus, and Ukraine. Around 988, Prince Vladimir of Kiev converted to Orthodox Christianity. Conversion also brought literacy to the Rus because the Bible was translated into a Slav language and written down in the Cyrillic alphabet still used in Russia today.

The Mongols

The unified state of Kiev collapsed in 1054 and was succeeded by a series of small, disunited states. In 1240, the Mongol or Tatar armies of Batu Khan, Genghis Khan's grandson, conquered the Rus lands, ruling them for more than 200 years as part of a vast Eurasian empire known as the Golden Horde. The Tatars exploited the Rus as slaves, recruiting them for their armies and exacting tribute from them each year. Although the Golden Horde failed to conquer Novgorod, the city paid tribute to the Mongols to keep its independence.

In 1240, Prince Alexander of Novgorod defeated the Swedes on the Neva River—hence his later

Alexander Nevsky, Prince of Novgorod (c. 1220–63), was renowned for his military victories in medieval Rus. He was canonized in the Russian Orthodox Church in 1547.

EARLY RULERS OF RUSSIA

Grand Princes of Moscow

1263–1303	Daniel
1303–25	Yuri
1325–41	Ivan I ("Moneybags")
1341–53	Simeon "the Proud"
1353–59	Ivan II, "the Meek"
1359–89	Dmitri Donskoi
1389–1425	Vasili I
1425–62	Vasili II

House of Rurik

1462–1505	Ivan III, "the Great"
1505–33	Vasili III
1533–84	Ivan IV, "the Terrible"
1584–98	Fyodor I

He inherited the throne in 1533, at the age of only three and was crowned in 1547 as "czar of all Russia," the first ruler to bear this title. He did much to reform and expand his state. In later life, however, he unleashed an orgy of violence against his boyars, or nobles, and those he suspected of plotting against him, killing tens of thousands in Novgorod and elsewhere.

Ivan "the Terrible" came to the throne of Russia in 1533 and ruled until his death in 1584. At first, he was a wise ruler and reformer, but later he waged war against his own subjects, massacring many people.

name "Nevsky"—and built up his country as an independent nation. Alexander was later canonized and has since become a great Russian hero.

The rise of Muscovy

In 1263, Alexander Nevsky's son Daniel became the first Grand Prince of Muscovy. At that time, Muscovy was a minor Russian state. In 1328, the Mongols recognized his son, Ivan I, as the most senior of the various Russian princes, while the Orthodox Church established Moscow as the center of Russian religion. Over the next two centuries, Muscovy expanded across central and northern Russia. Ivan III, the first of three Russian rulers to be called "the Great," started to call himself by the Roman title of czar, or Caesar, and claimed the inheritance of the former Orthodox Byzantine Empire, adopting its two-headed eagle as his emblem. He captured Novgorod by 1478 and ceased to pay tribute to the Tatars in 1480.

His grandson, Ivan "the Terrible," has gone down in history as a brutal, deranged tyrant.

THE RUSSIAN CZARS

House of Godunov

1598–1605	Boris Godunov
1605	Fyodor II

Usurpers

1605–06	"False" Dimitri I
1606–10	Vasili IV
1607–10	"False" Dimitri II
1610–13	Wladyslaw of Poland

The Romanovs

1613–45	Mikhail
1645–76	Aleksey
1676–82	Fyodor III
1682–96	Ivan V co-rules with Peter I
1682–1725	Peter I, "the Great"
1725–27	Catherine I
1727–30	Peter II
1730–40	Anna Ivanova
1740–41	Ivan VI
1741–61	Elizabeth Petrovna
1761–62	Peter III
1762–96	Catherine II, "the Great"
1796–1801	Paul I
1801–25	Alexander I
1825–55	Nicholas I
1855–81	Alexander II
1881–94	Alexander III
1894–1917	Nicholas II

The Time of Troubles

After his death in 1584, Ivan the Terrible was succeeded by his imbecilic son Fyodor I. The government was led by Boris Godunov, who became czar when Fyodor died, without an heir, in 1598. A series of bad harvests, famines, and an invasion by Poland weakened the country during the Time of Troubles, a period in which weak czars and false claimants struggled to seize the throne. In 1613, the Land Assembly of various social groups met to choose Mikhail Romanov as czar. His family would rule Russia until 1917.

The Romanovs

Under the first three Romanovs, Russia gained eastern Ukraine from Poland and expanded beyond the Urals into Siberia. The fourth Romanov, Peter the Great, was exceptional. He traveled to western Europe in search of new ideas to modernize his country, even studying

Peter the Great built St. Petersburg at the mouth of the Neva River on the Gulf of Finland, giving Russia maritime access to the Baltic Sea for the first time. Thousands died during its construction because the city was built on swampy ground.

When the Russian serfs, or peasants, were freed from the ownership and control of their landlords in 1861, they each received a small piece of land that they could farm for themselves. Yet the peasantry remained poor, as this photograph from 1917 shows.

shipbuilding in England. On his return, he defeated Sweden to gain control of the eastern Baltic and built a new European-style capital at St. Petersburg to give Russia a "window on the west." In 1721, he became the first czar to call himself an emperor.

Peter created Russia's first law of succession to the throne but then died in 1725 without choosing a successor. The rest of the century was dominated by the reigns of four empresses. Two of them, Elizabeth and Catherine the Great, were usurpers. Catherine the Great was in fact the German wife of Peter III, whom she ousted in a palace coup in 1762 and then killed. Two of the other three reigning male Romanovs were also assassinated, while Peter II died of smallpox at a young age. During this period, Russia continued its expansion west and south, gaining land from the Ottoman Empire and Poland.

Nineteenth-century Russia

By the start of the nineteenth century, Russia had become a major European power, although it almost lost its independence when Emperor Napoleon of France invaded in 1812. Russia continued its expansion south into central Asia and the Balkans, bringing it into continual conflict with the Ottoman Empire and, in 1854–56, Britain and France in the Crimea. Internally, however, the country was weak, and in 1825 the autocratic rule of the czars prompted a revolt. In 1861, Alexander II attempted to reform the country and freed the serfs, or peasants. He was assassinated in 1881, and his successor reinstated autocratic rule.

Revolution

Russian expansion east into Manchuria (today northeast China) led the country into a disastrous war with Japan in 1904–5. Russia's defeat led to a revolution against Nicholas II, after which he set up the first Russian *duma*, or parliament, albeit with limited powers. In 1914, Russia allied with Britain and France against Germany and Austria-Hungary at the start of World War I. The czar took personal control of the Russian army but was held responsible for military failures and for economic chaos. In February 1917, a shortage of bread in Petrograd (the renamed St. Petersburg) led to riots. Troops failed to intervene, and Nicholas II was forced to abdicate. The Romanov era had come to an end.

The Bolshevik Revolution

After the fall of the czar, a provisional government took power in Russia but continued the unpopular war against Germany. Committees of workers, many of them dominated by socialist and revolutionary parties opposed to the war, sprang up in industrial areas. In October 1917, one of the main revolutionary parties, the Bolsheviks, led by Vladimir Lenin, seized power in Petrograd. They signed a peace treaty with Germany but soon had to fight against anti-Bolshevik forces. The civil war lasted until the renamed Communist Party won in 1921.

Lenin was an inspired orator and revolutionary who set up the world's first communist state, taking all private property into state ownership.

The Soviet Union

In power, the communists carried out a political and social revolution, taking all industries and properties under state control and introducing equality between people by abolishing class differences. In 1922, Russia was reorganized to form the Union of Soviet Socialist Republics (USSR), which eventually contained the new Russian Federation as one of 15 republics, based around the major ethnic groups in the country.

After Lenin died in 1924, he was succeeded by Joseph Stalin, a ruthless leader who persecuted and killed millions of people opposed to his regime by execution or imprisonment in gulags (prison camps). Millions more were deported from their homelands or died during famines. Stalin introduced a series of five-year plans to take agriculture under state control and to industrialize the country.

World War II

In 1941, Nazi Germany invaded the USSR. The Nazis came close to capturing Moscow and

THE UNION OF SOVIET SOCIALIST REPUBLICS

Name	Size in sq mi	% of total USSR
Armenia	11,622	0.13
Azerbaijan	33,774	0.39
Belorussia*	80,964	0.93
Estonia	17,638	0.20
Georgia	27,183	0.31
Kazakhstan	1,063,647	12.24
Kirghizia*	77,415	0.89
Latvia	25,190	0.29
Lithuania	25,428	0.29
Moldavia	13,199	0.15
Russian Federation	6,659,328	76.62
Tajikistan	55,809	0.64
Turkmenistan	190,359	2.19
Ukraine	235,443	2.71
Uzbekistan	174,486	2.02

Note: 1 sq mi = 0.39 sq km
*Now Belarus and Kyrghyzstan.

Joseph Stalin (left) ran the USSR from 1924 until his death in 1953. He led the country to victory over Nazi Germany during World War II and, in 1945, met President Harry S. Truman (right) at Potsdam in Germany to decide the fate of post-war Europe.

besieged Leningrad (formerly Petrograd and St. Petersburg) for more than three years. They were eventually defeated in 1945 at the cost of at least 20 million Russian lives. The USSR regained western territories it had lost after the revolution and then controlled Eastern Europe. It set up a series of communist governments that ordered troops to suppress dissent in Hungary in 1956 and then again in Czechoslovakia in 1968.

The post-war world

Poor relations with its former wartime allies, notably the US, led to the Cold War—a war of propaganda and ideas in which the USSR tried to outpace the West. It developed nuclear weapons and intercontinental ballistic missiles, launched the first satellite and man into space and

competed economically and politically with the US. However, the USSR failed to deliver high living standards for its citizens and stagnated economically after the 1970s.

In 1985, Mikhail Gorbachev came to power. He attempted to reform the USSR through policies of glasnost (openness) and perestroika (reconstruction). He relaxed media censorship and urged people to debate their country's future.

Nationalists in the Baltic states and the Caucasus campaigned for independence. The Russian Federation, under Boris Yeltsin, also opposed Soviet control. In 1991, hard-line communists attempted to topple Gorbachev in a coup but were stopped by Yeltsin. The republics then declared their independence from the USSR, which collapsed at the end of 1991.

Mikhail Gorbachev attempted to reform the communist system from within while keeping the USSR intact, but rising nationalist tensions in a number of the 15 republics led to the end of communism and the collapse of the union.

The new order

The Russian Federation that emerged out of the wreckage of the former USSR lost much territory that had previously been part of the former Russian empire. It lost most of its coastline along the Baltic Sea to the three new independent states of Estonia, Latvia, and Lithuania and no longer contained Ukraine and Belarus, once the heartlands of the ancient Rus peoples. It also lost all its territory south of the Caucasus to three new republics and all of central Asia to another five new states. Where once there had been a single Soviet state, now there were 15 inheritors.

The breakup of the USSR created several immediate problems. The little Russian enclave of Kaliningrad on the Baltic—once part of German East Prussia and gained by Russia at the end of World War II—was now separated from the rest of Russia by Belarus, Latvia, and Lithuania. Millions of Russians found themselves living in foreign countries. Soviet nuclear weapons were stored not just in Russia but also in Belarus, Kazakhstan, and Ukraine, all three of which decided to scrap them. The cosmodrome of Baikonaur, where Soviet space missions were launched, was in Kazakhstan.

FOCUS: COMMONWEALTH OF INDEPENDENT STATES

As the USSR was breaking up in 1991, the leaders of Russia, Ukraine, and Belarus met to set up a loose successor organization, the Commonwealth of Independent States (CIS). The CIS has few powers beyond its national boundaries but coordinates trade, finance, security, lawmaking, and crime prevention between its member states. The CIS also sends troops to participate in United Nations (UN) peacekeeping missions. Twelve of the 15 former Soviet republics joined the CIS. Only the three Baltic states decided to remain outside, preferring to join the European Union (EU) in 2004. After Russia's military intervention in 2008, Georgia announced its decision to leave the CIS.

Boris Yeltsin became leader of the Russian Federation in 1990 and led the country to independence from the USSR in 1991. He oversaw the change from a communist to a capitalist economy.

Industries that once operated in a single country were now facing different currencies and tax rules.

Boris Yeltsin

The new government, with Boris Yeltsin as president of the Russian Federation, was immediately threatened by hard-line members of parliament opposed to reform. In December 1993, Yeltsin ordered tanks to bombard the Russian parliament. He also faced a battle in the Caucasus after the Russian republic of Chechnya declared independence. In 1994, Russian troops entered the country and fought a vicious war until peace was declared in 1996. In the economy, he sold off many of the state's shares in large industries, such as oil, aluminum, and mining. A few rich oligarchs made a lot of money, but in 1998, the economy collapsed. The currency, the rouble, was devalued, wages fell, inflation soared, and corruption flourished.

Vladimir Putin is the dominant figure in modern Russian politics, serving as president from 1999 to 2008 and prime minister since then. He has rebuilt Russia's economy, restricted the opposition, and pursued a hard-line foreign policy to protect Russia.

Putin and Medvedev

In 1999, Yeltsin handed over power to his chosen successor, Vladimir Putin. Putin was a former member of the KGB, the Soviet secret services, and was a far tougher president than Yeltsin. He cracked down on the oligarchs, strengthened the power of the state, and restricted the powers of the opposition. The rising price of oil and gas, two of Russia's main exports, made the country far richer than before and allowed Putin to rebuild the shattered economy. Putin won a second war in Chechnya and conducted a much more aggressive foreign policy in support of Russia's interests abroad. Putin won re-election in 2004 but was constitutionally forbidden from running for a third time as president in 2008. He continued in power, however, as prime minister under his chosen successor as president, Dmitry Medvedev.

CHAPTER 3

Social Changes

In 2002, the national census recorded that 145,166,731 people lived in Russia. The total fell by 532,000 in 2006 alone. While the rate of decline is slowing down, some experts believe the Russian population could fall about 40 million to a total of 100 million people by 2050, the same as it was in the early 1950s. That is one of the steepest falls in population of any country in the world and is occurring as the world's population rises from 6.6 billion in 2007 to around 9 billion by 2050.

The population drop

The main cause is the difference between birth and death rates. The birth rate is low, at 12.1 children per 1,000 people, while the death rate, at 14.7 people per 1,000, is high and rising. Russia has the biggest difference in life expectancy between women and men in the world.

RUSSIA'S DECLINING POPULATION

2002 census	145,166,731
2005 estimate	143,474,200
2009 estimate	141,903,979
2050 estimate	100,000,000

LIFE EXPECTANCY AT BIRTH IN YEARS

	2009	1989 (for USSR)
Men	59.3	64.6
Women	73.14	74
Difference	13.84	9.4

Source: 2002 Census and CIA *World Factbook*.

Homelessness is a problem in modern Russia because accommodation is in short supply and many people have no work. This elderly woman received a free meal during the cold winter of 2006.

The main reasons behind these statistics are poor health, poor health care, and poverty. More than 40,000 Russians died of alcohol poisoning in 2003, with many more dying from alcohol-related illnesses, heart disease, cancer, or industrial and other accidents. Russian men are heavy smokers, with 61 percent of those age 18 and over smoking. Only 15 percent of Russian women smoke. HIV rates, especially among drug users, are high and rising. Nearly two-thirds of Russian children are considered to be unhealthy, while more than 35 percent of all Russians live in poverty, a major cause of ill health. Russia has one of the highest suicide rates in the world, with 32.2 deaths per 1,000 of the population, six out of seven of whom are men. The health care system is underfunded and often runs short of drugs and medical supplies. Under communism, the state-owned enterprises provided generous health care for their workers, but the new private companies are not so generous, and health and welfare provision is increasingly restricted.

Most Russians live in modern high-rise blocks. Accommodation is often crowded, with extended families of two or three generations living together in two-room apartments.

Family living

Most young people get married between the ages of 18 and 24, but few live in their own apartment or house. A shortage of housing means that most couples live with an extended family of grandparents, parents, aunts, uncles, brothers, and sisters. The vast majority of Russians live in high-rise blocks of small apartments. An average Russian has 177 square feet (16.4 sq m) of living space compared with 646 square feet (60 sq m) for the average American. About 5.5 million people live in the old-style *komunalki*. These are communal flats where families live in one room and share the kitchen and bathroom with other families. *Komunalki* are reserved for the poor but are increasingly being converted by rich Russians into large, single-family apartments.

Russian women

In the Russian language, *rodina* (homeland) is a feminine word. Russians call their country "Mother Russia" and speak of the "motherland." Women and motherhood have always been important in Russian society, but the role of women is changing today.

Communist roles

Under communism, women were given full equality with men and had rights that were unequaled anywhere else in the world. The state provided them with free child day care and required men to provide child support if a couple got divorced. Women worked in factories, farms, and the professions. Many fought in World War II as pilots of bombers and fighter planes.

In practice, however, women remained unequal. Few women entered politics. In the entire history of the USSR, only three women sat on the ruling Politburo, the chief decision-making committee of the Communist Party, and almost none achieved high roles in the diplomatic service or the military. Despite what was recorded in the Soviet constitution, women were mainly expected to be good wives and mothers, caring for their children, giving birth to future Soviet citizens, and being responsible for the day-to-day chores around the home.

WOMEN FACT FILE

Total number: 77,561,598 (2002 census)

Percentage of population: 53.5%

Life expectancy: 73.14 years (2009)

Percentage of labor force: 52%

Percentage of college graduates: 62%

Number of women in parliament: 63 out of 450, or 14% (2009)

Women government ministers: 3 out of 26, or 11.6% (2009)

Source: 2002 Census and CIA *World Factbook*.

This Soviet poster from 1935 shows women driving trucks, with factories in the background. Women were expected to participate fully in the economy, yet despite their major role, they did not gain any political power.

In 2004, Irina Khakamada ran for election as president of Russia. She was the only woman out of the six candidates. She ran as an independent and fierce critic of Vladimir Putin but came in fourth in the final poll with 3.84 percent of the total vote.

Modern women

The post-communist 1993 constitution confirmed the equality of women with men, but since then, women have both advanced and slipped back. Today, Russian women outnumber men by about 10 million, due to their better health and longer life expectancy. About 62 percent of Russian women are college graduates, compared to just half of men, and the majority of middle- and high-ranking professionals are women. Women are especially well represented in medicine, making up 75 percent of all doctors. In education, they make up 80 percent of school principals and most teachers. Women are also increasingly entering politics, getting elected as local and national politicians and serving as government ministers, although not in large numbers.

Despite these advances, life remains tough for many women. A woman's average salary is only two-thirds that of a man, and women are more likely to be let go if a firm is cutting jobs. Traditional male views mean that many women face sexual harassment at work and violence at home. Official statistics record that 14,000 women a year are killed by their husbands or boyfriends. The police rarely intervene in domestic disputes, and few women go to the law to protect their rights. The family, traditionally the center of a Russian woman's life, is undergoing great change. The divorce rate is rising, with half of all marriages now ending this way. In 2000, one-third of all children were born to unmarried mothers, double the number a decade before, and two out of three pregnancies end in abortion.

Women view their changing circumstances in different ways. Some wish to remain wives and mothers and believe their place is in the home. Others want to play a part in Russian life, running businesses, entering politics, and playing a full role in modern society. Unlike much of Europe, feminism has had little impact in Russia, with women still more likely to be regarded by men as less than equal citizens.

Most Russian newspapers support the government—few dare to criticize leaders or policies. The state owns both national television channels, making it difficult for Russians to access independent news and opinion.

The media

Under the communists, the media was tightly controlled. The state owned all newspapers and radio and television stations and closely monitored their contents. Books were checked to make sure they contained nothing the state disapproved of. Foreign radio and television stations were blocked from broadcasting into the USSR, and foreign newspapers and books were heavily censored or banned.

Censorship was relaxed under Gorbachev and then abolished after the collapse of the USSR. A range of independent radio and television services began broadcasting, new newspapers appeared, and publishing houses began to print books that had previously been banned or unavailable. However, while the media

FOCUS: RUSSAN JOURNALISM

In modern Russia, newspapers favor the government, and many critical editorial staff and journalists have been fired. Most worryingly, 49 journalists have been murdered since 1992, notably the high-profile writer Anna Politkovskaya (right), gunned down in her apartment block in 2006, possibly on the orders of Chechen leaders, who disliked her investigative reports into their human rights abuses. In 2007, the Worldwide Press Freedom Index listed Russia as one of the most dangerous places for a journalist to work and ranked it 140 out of 167 countries (the most dangerous place is North Korea, at 167).

has more freedom, it is by no means as free as it is in the rest of Europe. Under Putin and Medvedev, the state has re-emerged as the main controller of the media. The two main national television stations are both state owned, and reports are biased in favour of the government.

Many Russians access news through foreign cable and satellite stations such as CNN and BBC Worldwide or through the *runet*, which is the Russian Internet. Foreign news magazines, such as the *Economist* and *Newsweek*, are widely available in the cities, as are English-language newspapers in Moscow and St. Petersburg. There is also a flourishing and independent magazine and book publishing industry.

Russian education

One of the great legacies of communist rule was a state education system that delivered almost total adult literacy. Russian schooling is free and compulsory from age six to 15, with 68 percent of students going on to higher education. The old centralized communist system, in which the state controlled the curriculum and textbooks were the same throughout the country, was replaced in 1992 by a new system. This was run by local authorities and allowed teachers more flexibility over what and how they taught. Soviet-era textbooks were rewritten, school uniforms were no longer compulsory, and military training was removed from the curriculum, although President Putin reinstated it in 2000. Under the new system, private schools are allowed, with many of them run by the Orthodox Church.

The Russian Federation inherited a well-developed education system from the USSR. More recently, funding to schools has declined, as have teachers' wages. Many senior teachers have left education for other, better-paid sectors.

Religion

Under communism, the Russian Orthodox Church and other religions were suppressed. Hundreds of thousands of priests, monks, nuns, and Muslim imams were killed. People were imprisoned for attending religious services, and organized religion was considered anti-Soviet.

The arrival of perestroika under the reforming government of Mikhail Gorbachev in the 1980s changed the situation drastically. Churches re-opened, congregations grew, and young men re-entered the priesthood. Today, the Russian Orthodox Church plays a major role in national life. Many couples marry in church and baptize their children, although church attendance is more often a social event than a religous one. Islam is strong in the south, and there are Buddhist, Shamanist, and Jewish communities living throughout Russia. A lasting legacy of communism is a large number of atheists.

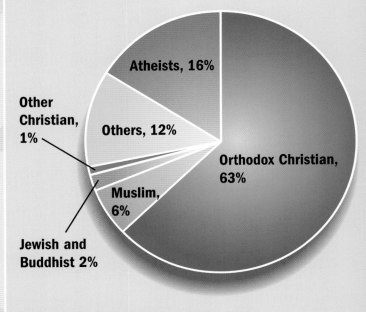

Religious beliefs

Atheists, 16%
Other Christian, 1%
Others, 12%
Orthodox Christian, 63%
Muslim, 6%
Jewish and Buddhist 2%

Source: Russian Public Opinion Research Center, 2007

About two-thirds of Russians claim to be Orthodox Christians, although church observance is strong only among the elderly. Although Russia is technically a secular state, a law passed in 1997 recognizes Judaism Christianity, Islam, Buddhism, and other beliefs.

The post-communist constitution separates the church and state, but under the Putin and Medvedev governments, the Russian Orthodox Church has drawn closer to the state.

St. Basil's Cathedral in Red Square, Moscow, was commissioned by Czar Ivan the Terrible to commemorate the capture of the Khanate of Kazan from the Tatars in 1552. Its onion-shaped domes are typical of Russian Orthodox churches.

Muslims, seen here at prayer in the Central Mosque in Moscow, number about 9 million. Most live in the major cities or in the Caucasus region in the south.

The Russian Orthodox Church feels threatened by the rise of other Christian religions, most notably Catholicism and Pentecostalism. The government recognizes the "special role" of the church in Russian history and sees it as one of the main institutions that binds the new Russia together. As a result, the government has intervened on the church's behalf in property conflicts with other faiths. It has smothered other faiths with new laws and unnecessary bureaucracy that restrict their activities and their ability to build new churches.

Crime

The end of harsh communist rule resulted in a massive rise in crime, which doubled between 1985 and 1992 and has continued to rise ever since. Violent crime and robberies are common, as is corruption and fraud at all levels of public and commercial life. Computer hacking is also rife. In 2008, the annual corruption index compiled by Transparency International, a Berlin-based group that highlights international corruption, placed Russia 147 out of 180 countries. The US ranked 18, Britain, 16, and Denmark, New Zealand, and Sweden were all first as the least corrupt nations of all countries.

Organized gangs operate in many cities, running protection rackets and dealing in prostitution, money laundering, smuggling and drugs. A new, Russian-style Mafia of gangsters and racketeers, often organized along ethnic lines, has moved in to grab a share of the vast oil and mineral wealth. Turf wars between the gangs are common. Rising Russian nationalism has also led to an increase in skinhead gangs linked to the neo-Nazi movement or attached to soccer clubs that target Jews, immigrants, gays, blacks, and others they consider to be non-Russian. As a result, Russia has one of the highest murder rates, in the world, with 22 murders for every 100,000 people. This compares to the rate in the US of 5.5 per 100,000.

CHAPTER 4

Political Changes

The head of state of the Russian Federation is the president, directly elected by the people to serve for four years. After 2012, however, the new president will serve for six years. Currently, the president is forbidden by the constitution from serving more than two consecutive terms. This is why, in 2008, President Vladimir Putin stepped down from office—he had served two terms as president since being elected in 2000. The current president is Dmitry Medvedev.

The president is both the formal head of state and the head of government as well as commander in chief of the armed forces. He sets the basic direction of Russian domestic and foreign policies, appoints ambassadors, signs international treaties and represents Russia when he travels abroad.

The executive

The president has the power to appoint a prime minister, currently the former president, Vladimir Putin. The prime minister heads a cabinet of ministers consisting of two first-deputy and six deputy prime ministers. There are also 17 departmental ministers in charge of areas such as health, justice, and culture. The prime minister and his team run the executive branch of government—the branch that administers the country, enforces law, and provides services such as police, passport control, and pensions.

The Kremlin in Moscow was the ancient fortified palace of the czars and has been the center of Soviet and now Russian government ever since the national capital moved back from St. Petersburg in 1918.

The legislative

The legislative, or lawmaking part of government, is the Federal Assembly. It consists of two chambers, the 450-member State Duma, or lower house, and the 168-member Federation Council, or upper house.

The Duma is elected every four years (every five years after 2011) by adult voters age 21 and over. Seats in the Duma are awarded by proportional representation, which means according to the national percentage of votes won by each party. The party selects candidates to fill its eligible number of seats. A party must win 7 percent of the national vote to be represented in the Duma. In 2007, seven minor parties failed to win any seats. The Duma approves laws and the annual budget, approves the appointment of the prime minister, and oversees

The State Duma is the lower house of the Russian parliament and has 450 elected members.

the work of government departments, the central bank, and other organizations. It also has the power to vote no confidence in the government, forcing it to resign.

The Federation Council consists of 166 senators, two from each of the 83 federal subjects, or districts, of Russia. One of the two senators is chosen by the provincial parliament, the other by the provincial governor. Political parties and factions are forbidden in the council, which makes its work much more consensual. The role of the council is to work with the Duma to pass laws, approve presidential decrees, and legal appointments, and, if necessary, approve the impeachment or removal from office of the president if he has failed in his job.

A proposed law starts life in the Duma and is then passed to the Federation Council. The council cannot change the law but can either approve or reject it. If it rejects it, the two chambers form a joint commission to agree to a compromise. If that fails, the Duma can override the council's veto with a two-thirds-majority vote.

2007 DUMA ELECTIONS

Party	% of vote	Seats
United Russia: the governing party	64.3	315
Communist Party: the former ruling party of the USSR	11.6	57
Liberal Democratic Party: a Russian nationalist party	8.1	40
Fair Russia: a conservative party	7.7	38
Seven other small parties	8.3	0
Total		450
Turnout (63.1%)	69,537,065	
Electorate	109,145,517	

Source: Russian Election Commission

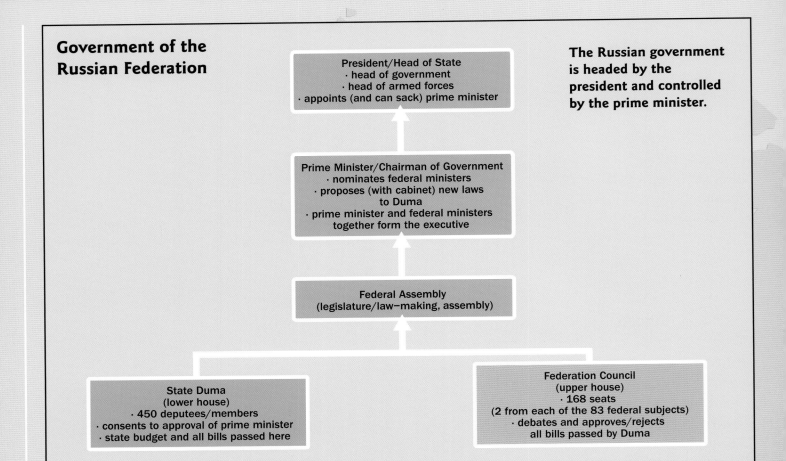

Government of the Russian Federation

President/Head of State
· head of government
· head of armed forces
· appoints (and can sack) prime minister

Prime Minister/Chairman of Government
· nominates federal ministers
· proposes (with cabinet) new laws to Duma
· prime minister and federal ministers together form the executive

Federal Assembly
(legislature/law–making, assembly)

State Duma
(lower house)
· 450 deputees/members
· consents to approval of prime minister
· state budget and all bills passed here

Federation Council
(upper house)
· 168 seats
(2 from each of the 83 federal subjects)
· debates and approves/rejects all bills passed by Duma

The Russian government is headed by the president and controlled by the prime minister.

The Federation

The Russian Federation consists of 83 federal subjects, or districts, divided into six different types according to the amount of power they have. The most common are the 46 *oblasts* (regions), each with a federally appointed governor and a locally elected legislature. Then there are 21 autonomous (self-governing) republics, each with its own president, parliament, and constitution. Republics are home to a particular ethnic group and are allowed to have an official language alongside Russian. The republic best known to the outside world is Chechnya in the Caucasus region.

There are another nine *krais* (territories) that are much like the *oblasts*. Within the *krais* are autonomous *okrugs* (districts) and an autonomous *oblast*: they are subordinate to the *krais* of which they form a part. The two main

Russian cities of Moscow and St. Petersburg are administered as federal cities.

Political reality

On paper, Russia has a constitution much like any other democratic nation. Elections take place, parliament passes laws, the president and prime minister are held to account for their actions, and the people take part in a working democracy that

THE RUSSIAN FEDERATION

Federal subjects:	83, of which:
Oblasts (regions)	46
Republics	21
Krais (territories)	9
Autonomous *okrugs* (districts)	4
Autonomous *oblasts*	1
Federal cities	2

has a say in the government of their state. However, the reality is quite different.

Ever since the new constitution was passed in 1993, power has flowed towards the president, so much so that modern Russia is now midway between democracy and one-person rule. This change was promoted by Vladimir Putin when he was president. Although Putin is now prime minister, he still has great power behind the scenes.

Controlling the government

The president appoints the prime minister. Through the prime minister, he appoints the government and, since 2005, all 83 regional governors. This gives the president control over the national and regional governments and over the Federation Council because regional governors appoint half its membership. Most importantly, the president controls the Duma. When he was president, Vladimir Putin promoted the United Russia Party, of which he is chairman, as the main political party in Russia. He made sure rival parties could not get elected to the Duma by

placing legal obstacles in their way to stop them from forming and registering for elections. He also tightened control over the media to deny opposition parties airtime.

In 2005, the electoral system was changed from one in which half the Duma was directly elected to a wholly proportional system. This meant that well-known individuals could not run for election as independents but had to join a political party. The threshold for electing parties was also changed, rising from 5 percent to 7 percent of the total vote. This meant that regional parties were unlikely to get elected.

In the 2007 Duma elections, 14 parties were eligible to run. Three were ruled out of order for various reasons, and seven failed to gain more than 7 percent of the vote. Thus, only four political parties are currently represented in the Duma. But such is Putin's control over politics that two of the opposition parties, the Liberal Democrats and Fair Russia, support his own United Russia Party. Putin therefore commands 412 of the 450 seats in the Duma, with only the Communist Party opposing his government.

Russian police break up a march in April 2007 led by Gary Kasparov, the former Russian world chess champion, opposing Putin's government.

CHAPTER 5
Economic and Environmental Changes

Under communist rule, every Russian factory, workshop, iron- and steelworks, coal mine, car assembly line, department store, and shop was owned by the state on behalf of the people. There was no private ownership of production lines or of distribution. Everything in the economy was controlled and directed through a series of one- and five-year economic plans. Each factory, workshop, and farm was given production targets it had to meet. The state directed where investment in new machinery or products was to go to meet those targets. The state also set the prices of every product sold in Russia, from a barrel of oil and a new car to a pair of shoes and a loaf of bread.

This rigorous control and planning of every aspect of the economy did have some positive effects because it meant that everyone had a job and poverty was largely abolished. But the system was too rigid and unresponsive to what people wanted to buy and own. Quality was poor, choice was limited, and, in comparison to Western economies, goods were old-fashioned. Factories were inefficient and polluting, and managers and workers did not take any initiatives to make things better unless the plan directed them to.

The USSR became a major car manufacturer, but prices were high and quality was low. Soviet industry was inefficient and costly and largely unresponsive to people's needs.

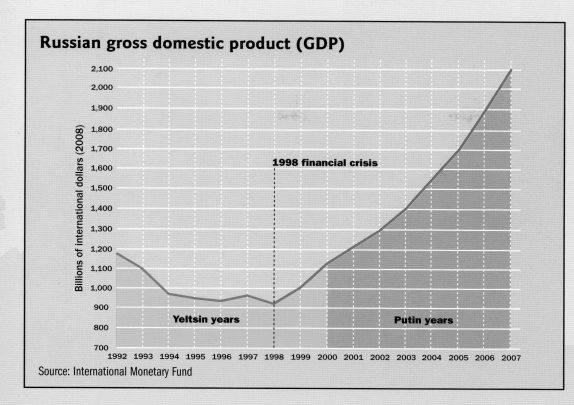

Russian gross domestic product (GDP)

1998 financial crisis

Yeltsin years

Putin years

Billions of international dollars (2008)

2,100
2,000
1,900
1,800
1,700
1,600
1,500
1,400
1,300
1,200
1,100
1,000
900
800
700

1992 1993 1994 1995 1996 1997 1998 1999 2000 2001 2002 2003 2004 2005 2006 2007

Source: International Monetary Fund

The Russian economy boomed during the Putin years. Russia's total wealth increased significantly as its economy rose from twenty-second to eighth largest in the world by 2008.

Reforming the system

In the late 1980s, President Gorbachev began to reform the system but had little success. Then in October 1991, Boris Yeltsin announced radical reforms to transform the economy from a centrally planned state-run economy to a Western-style free market economy. He scrapped central planning and removed price controls. Most controversially, he sold off state-owned industries at bargain basement prices to business tycoons, the so-called "oligarchs." These oligarchs made fortunes and gained considerable political influence through ownerships of key industries. Other industries fell into the hands of organized crime.

The Yeltsin reforms quickly produced hyperinflation (a massive rise in prices). In 1992, prices rose by 2,520 percent. The economy collapsed, many people lost their jobs and savings, and many more were plunged into poverty. The government acted to control prices, and by 1997, the economy had improved. However, a financial crisis in 1998 led to a collapse in the value of the rouble and the stock market crashed. Many of the gains of previous years were wiped out, and people lost all their savings as banks collapsed and inflation rose.

After the trauma of Yelstin's reforms and the crash of 1998, the economy began to improve under President Putin. Rising international prices for oil and gas, Russia's biggest exports, brought wealth to the country. Inflation fell, investment in new factories and equipment rose by 125 percent, and industrial production rose by 75 percent.

Real incomes more than doubled and the average monthly salary rose from $80 to $480. As a result, the economy has grown by an average of 7 percent a year since 2000. By 2007, the Russian economy had recovered from the losses incurred since the economic transformation began in 1991. Under Putin, the Russian economy rose from twenty-second to eleventh largest in the world. By 2008, it had risen to eighth place, ahead of Spain, Brazil, Canada, and India but behind the United Kingdom, France, Germany, China, Japan, and the US, which is in first place.

The modern economy

Russia has many economic strengths. It has vast reserves of oil, natural gas, and coal and of gold, other minerals, and raw materials such as timber. Its fishing industry is the fourth largest in the world behind Japan, the US and China. It is the world's leading arms manufacturer and a major producer of nuclear power plants. It is also a leading computer software and information technology systems designer, producer, and exporter. Its space program launches commercial satellites, and its civilian aerospace industry is developing a new range of passenger jets. Importantly for the future, Russia has a highly educated workforce, with more students in higher education than at any time in its history.

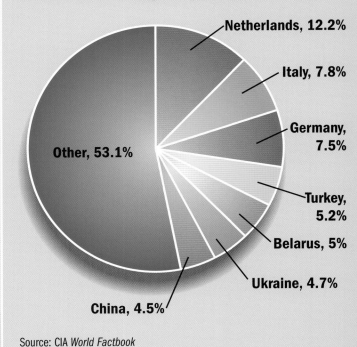

Russia's main export partners, 2007

- Netherlands, 12.2%
- Italy, 7.8%
- Germany, 7.5%
- Turkey, 5.2%
- Belarus, 5%
- Ukraine, 4.7%
- China, 4.5%
- Other, 53.1%

Source: CIA *World Factbook*

Russia exports oil, natural gas, chemicals, metals, wood, military equipment, and manufactured goods around the world. Most of its exports go to China and its near neighbors in Europe.

However, the economy still faces many problems. Much of its industrial equipment is old and outdated, and there has not been enough investment to improve it. Its legal and financial systems are still not adequate to deal with the new type of economy Russia is developing. Too many of the new firms are monopolies without any competitors to make them more efficient. Above all, Russia is too reliant on exports of oil and natural gas. About half of the national budget revenue comes from taxes and customs duties on exports and home sales of oil and gas. This makes Russia vulnerable if the price of oil drops around the world or if the world economy shrinks and does not require so much energy.

Today, the Russian Federal Space Agency (Roscosmos) leases the cosmodrome in Baikonaur from the Kazakh government. From there, it launches commercial telecommunications and weather satellites into orbit.

Russia exports more than 5 million barrels per day of oil to European markets, mainly through terminals such as this one near St. Petersburg.

The 2009 crash

The world economic crash of 2008–9 hit Russia very hard. As the world's economy went into recession, the price of a barrel of Russian oil dropped from $147 in July 2008 to about $45 by mid-2009. The Moscow stock market crashed, foreign exchange reserves (the amount of gold, foreign currencies, and other assets held by the Russian central bank) more than halved, and a number of small banks failed. Although this crisis started in the US and affected the rest of the world, Russia was very hard hit, mainly because its economy is not yet strong enough to resist such shocks.

Coping with change

The impact of rapid economic change has been felt by the ordinary person in Russia. The older generation, brought up under the certainties and fixed prices of communism, finds the new economic situation very confusing. Pensions are now worth little as inflation remains high, while those still working find their wages fail to keep up with rising prices. Many managers and workers find the new challenges of a market economy difficult to cope with. Under communism, they carried out the orders of the national plan, but now they must be dynamic and make decisions for themselves. This is difficult for those who are used to being told what to do. Younger people find these changes easier to deal with. Unlike their parents, many of them have traveled abroad and have seen what a rich market economy looks like in practice. They did not experience life under the communists and are very open to new ideas.

Imports from China, South Korea, Japan, and Western Europe mainly consist of vehicles, machinery and other engineering equipment, iron, steel, plastics, medicines, consumer goods, and foodstuffs.

Russia's main import partners, 2007

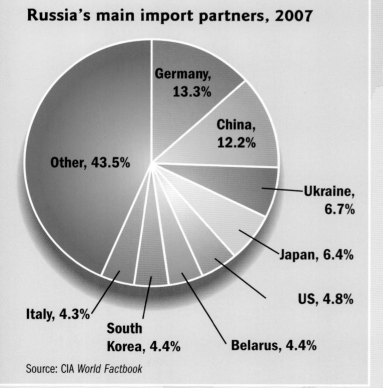

Germany, 13.3%
China, 12.2%
Other, 43.5%
Ukraine, 6.7%
Japan, 6.4%
US, 4.8%
Italy, 4.3%
South Korea, 4.4%
Belarus, 4.4%

Source: CIA *World Factbook*

Smoke from a steel plant belches carbon monoxide into the sky above the city of Novokuznetsk in Siberia. By the early 1990s, every major river in Russia was polluted and one-quarter of all drinking water unsafe to consume.

industrial landscapes in the world. Constant air pollution from heavy industries, carbon emissions from coal-fired electricity power stations and cars, industrial and agricultural pollution of rivers, lakes, and seacoasts, contaminated groundwater from toxic waste, soil contamination from agricultural pesticides, soil erosion from insensitive agriculture, and deforestation have all had a detrimental effect on the environment and on people's health.

Despite this record, green issues are not high on the political agenda, and there is no active political green movement. The Russian government has signed international agreements, such as the Kyoto Protocol on climate change, but there is still little political will or resources to tackle this major problem.

The environment

In their desire to make the USSR a major economic power, the communists concentrated on mass industrial production with little concern for the environment. Chimneys belched out smoke and dust, chemical works tipped poisonous wastes straight into local rivers, and toxic waste was often dumped untreated in landfill sites.

The result of years of environmental neglect is that Russia has one of the most heavily polluted

The nuclear issue

Soviet Russia was the second country after the US to test and produce nuclear weapons, later developing a large civilian nuclear power industry.

Russia, however, has a poor safety record in its nuclear industry and, like other countries, is struggling to devise safe methods to treat and store nuclear waste.

When the USSR collapsed, its nuclear arsenal of weapons was spread across Ukraine, Belarus, and Kazakhstan as well as Russia itself. The three new countries decided to get rid of these weapons, sending most of them back to Russia. In the chaotic collapse of the USSR, perhaps up to 100 of these weapons disappeared, although some politicians have put the figure as high as 250.

In 1986, a Soviet nuclear power station blew up at Chernobyl in the then Soviet republic of Ukraine. This became the worst-ever nuclear accident in history. The fallout contaminated large parts of neighboring Belarus and led to many civilian deaths from cancers in later years.

CASE STUDY: LAKE BAIKAL

Lake Baikal, the "Pearl of Siberia," is a UNESCO World Heritage Site and one of the world's most important natural environments. It is home to more than 1,700 species of plants and animals. Two-thirds of these are unique to the lake. Despite its importance, the lake has been badly treated. For 40 years, it was polluted by a paper mill that used chlorine to bleach its paper and then discharged the untreated waste directly into the water. The plant closed in 2008. Today, the government is pressing ahead with a uranium enrichment center whose radioactive and toxic materials can contaminate freshwater. Increased tourism and industrial activity in the region also threaten the lake.

CHAPTER 6

Changing Relationships

In the past century, the role of Russia has changed in the world. The USSR played a major part in the defeat of Nazi Germany during World War II and emerged at the end of the war in 1945 as one of the world's two superpowers, along with the US. These two countries engaged in the long Cold War, fighting each other with ideas and propaganda until the collapse of communism in 1991. They each built up huge nuclear arsenals and massive armies, conducted a race into space, and tried to establish political dominance throughout the rest of the world, with far-reaching consequences.

Rebuilding the Union

After the collapse of the USSR, the new Russia was economically weak. It relied on the West for economic and technical support. Under Yeltsin, Russia began to move nearer the West both politically and economically. That move went into reverse under Putin and Medvedev. Putin is a strong admirer of the former USSR, calling its collapse "the greatest geopolitical catastrophe" of the twentieth century.

Prime Minister Putin (right) and President Medvedev (left) have both pursued aggressive foreign policies to restore Russian dominance over former Soviet republics.

Russia has therefore tried to reestablish its dominance over the 14 independent republics that were once part of the Russian and Soviet empires. It regards these republics as within its traditional sphere of influence and dislikes Western involvement in these countries. Russia has maintained close links with Belarus and many of the central Asian republics but bitterly resents the fact that the three Baltic states of Estonia, Latvia, and Lithuania have turned to the West and joined the European Union (EU) and the North Atlantic Treaty Organization (NATO).

Poor relations

Russia also resented the pro-democracy Orange Revolution in Ukraine, which toppled the pro-

In 2008, the Georgian government attempted to regain control of its rebel, pro-Russian province of South Ossetia. The Russian government responded by sending in troops to support the rebels. Russian troops still occupy South Ossetia today.

Russian president in favor of a pro-Western candidate in 2004. More recently, in 2008, Putin's successor, Medvedev, sent troops into Georgia, in the Caucasus region, supposedly to protect the Russian minority in the Georgian province of South Ossetia but in reality to destabilize the anti-Russian, pro-Western Georgian government. Russia still occupies South Ossetia and the province of Abkhazia and has declared them independent. Moreover, Russia is expanding its military presence in these areas.

Russia and the West

The biggest change in Russia's relationships is with Western democracies. After the collapse of communism, Russia expected the old Cold War division of democratic Western and communist Eastern Europe to end and their separate military alliances to be wound up. But while the Warsaw Pact collapsed in the East, the West kept NATO and has since expanded it to include the Baltic states and many former communist countries in Eastern Europe. Russia is therefore faced with a potentially hostile military alliance right on its borders. The possibility of Ukraine and Georgia joining NATO—and also the EU—has added to the tension. So too has a US proposal to site missile defense shields in Poland and the Czech Republic, supposedly to block missiles from Iran. Russia regards this as a hostile act and has

Two wars in Chechnya in 1994–96 and again in 1999–2000 have reduced its capital, Grozny, to rubble. Russian troops fought separatist fighters, with both sides committing widespread human rights violations.

threatened to deploy intercontinental missiles with multiple warheads in response.

Russia resents intervention by Western democracies in its domestic affairs, in particular criticism of its human rights record in Chechnya, a republic that lies in the northern Caucasus. It also dislikes the accusation that its government has restricted opposition participation in recent elections. This feeling of resentment and annoyance is contributing to the increasingly tense relationship Russia has with the West.

EUROPEAN DEPENDENCE ON RUSSIAN GAS, 2009

Russia's major European customers dependent on Russian gas include

Bulgaria	100%
Finland	100%
Slovakia	100%
Greece	90%
Czech Republic	75%
Hungary	65%
Turkey	60%
Austria	51%
Poland	40%
Germany	37%
Italy	25%

Source: www.russiatoday.com/Top_News/2009-01-14/
European_dependence_on_Russian_gas.html

Gas supply

Russia has 32 percent of the world's natural gas reserves and is the world's biggest exporter of this resource. It uses gas as a bargaining tool against its neighbors. Russian gas—and gas from central Asian republics such as Turkmenistan—flows in Russian-owned pipelines through Ukraine and Belarus, keeping much of Europe warm in the winter. On a number of occasions, Russia has cut the gas supply to Ukraine, supposedly because Ukraine has not paid its large gas bill but more probably as a way of keeping Ukraine in check. Ukraine has responded by syphoning off gas destined for Europe, causing 18 countries in central Europe and the Balkans to suffer in the winter of 2008–9. Recently, Russia has proposed building a new pipeline from Russia along the Baltic Sea floor to Germany, bypassing Poland, a

strong critic of Russia. In response, the EU has proposed the Nabucco pipeline, which will transport gas from central Asia via Turkey to central Europe, bypassing Russia altogether. The EU fears Russia will use its stranglehold on gas supplies to influence its neighbors, notably Ukraine and Poland, while Russia fears that in trying to obtain supplies from central Asia, the EU is undermining its position in the region.

When Russia cut off gas supplies to Ukraine in 2008, it caused supplies in Eastern and Central Europe to be cut off as well. Residents of Sofia, the capital of Bulgaria, had to collect firewood to heat their homes.

CHAPTER 7

Future Challenges

Russia faces considerable challenges in the future, but so do its neighbors. How will Russia develop in the future, and how will that development affect its neighbours and the wider world?

Russia at home

Modern Russia has many advantages over most other countries. It is entirely self-sufficient in energy and will remain so for many years. It has vast natural resources of almost every mineral, many of which lie untapped and even undiscovered beneath Siberia and the Arctic Ocean. It has a good transportation infrastructure, and while its industry is often poorly equipped, new investment is upgrading many factories and plants. It also has a well-educated workforce.

This photograph shows the Russian military marching in Red Square, Moscow, during the annual Victory Day parade to celebrate the end of World War II. The size and strength of the Russian armed forces increasingly alarms Russia's neighbors.

The Russian company Gazprom is the largest extractor of natural gas in the world. It is the largest company in Russia and is so rich that it contributes about one-quarter of all national tax revenues.

On the downside, crime is very high and respect for the law is low. Housing is limited, and for most people what is available is cramped and of poor quality. Environmental safeguards are inadequate, and pollution is high. The standard of health and of health care remains very poor.

Russian government

The biggest issue facing future Russia is its style of government. Although technically a democracy, Russia is in fact a "managed democracy"—an authoritarian state governed by a strong president and prime minister and run by a few very rich oligarchs. The people running Russia also own large parts of it. For example, former KGB spy Igor Sechin is both deputy prime minister in charge of energy and chairs the board of Rosneft, Russia's largest oil company. Another former spy, Sergei Naryshkin, is chief of the presidential administration but also on the board of a shipping company and chairman of Channel One, Russia's main TV station.

Under Putin, human rights have been ignored and democracy curtailed. Although Putin stepped down as president in 2008 to become prime minister, there is nothing to stop him from returning as president in 2012, this time for two six-year terms. He is supported by the media, unlike his opponents, and Russia has seen significant economic growth under his leadership, all of which helps his popularity ratings.

Russia abroad

A strong Russia presents problems abroad, particularly to those former Soviet republics, such

as Ukraine and Georgia, on its borders. Russia has already used its energy supplies to threaten Ukraine and could do the same to Europe in the future. Many political commentators see a new cold war starting between Russia and the West. The old cold war, which lasted from the end of World War II in 1945 to the collapse of communism in 1991, was fought with ideas and propaganda, backed up by the threat of nuclear war. The new cold war will be fought with natural resources. Where once the Soviet Red Army was a threat, now it is the Russian gas company Gazprom and its ability to switch off Europe's supply of gas. Future Russia will present a strong challenge to the rest of the world.

Timeline

862 Novgorod invites Rurik the Varangian to rule the Rus.

882 Prince Oleg occupies Kiev.

c. 988 Prince Vladimir of Kiev converts to Christianity.

1169 Rus capital moves to Vladimir.

1237–40 Mongol (Tatar) armies attack and eventually sack Kiev, Vladimir, and other cities and establish empire of the Golden Horde.

1240 Alexander Nevsky of Novgorod defeats the Swedes at the Neva River.

1263 Daniel becomes first Grand Prince of Muscovy.

1326 Seat of Russian Orthodoxy moves from Vladimir to Moscow.

1328 Tatars recognize Ivan I as senior Rus prince.

1462 Ivan III calls himself czar or Caesar; he marries niece of last Byzantine emperor and claims Muscovy as inheritor of Byzantium and main center of Orthodoxy.

1478 Muscovy conquers Novgorod.

1480 Muscovy shakes off Tatar rule.

1533–84 Reign of Ivan IV, "the Terrible."

1547 Ivan is crowned first "czar of all Russia."

1552 Ivan conquers southern khanates of Kazan and later Astrakahan, giving Russia access to the Caspian Sea.

1613 Mikhail is chosen as first Romanov czar.

1667 Russia gains Kiev from Poland.

1682–1725 Reign of Peter I, "the Great."

1712 Seat of government moves from Moscow to St. Petersburg.

1721 Russia gains Baltic coastline from Sweden.

1721 Peter takes title "Emperor of all Russia."

1762–96 Reign of Catherine II, "the Great."

1772–93 Russia gains much of eastern Poland.

1783 Russia gains the Crimea.

1812 French Emperor Napoleon invades Russia but fails to conquer.

1815 Russia acquires rest of Poland.

1825 Decembrist revolt of liberal army officers against Nicholas I fails.

1854–56 Crimean War against Britain, France, and Ottoman Empire.

1859 Russia completes conquest of the northern Caucasus.

1861 Alexander I liberates the serfs.

1867 Russia sells Alaska to the United States.

1881 Alexander II is assassinated and succeeded by Alexander III, who clamps down on dissent.

1884 Russia completes conquest of central Asia.

1891–1916 Trans-Siberian Railway built.

1904–5 War with Japan.

1905 Revolution leads to constitutional reform.

1914 Russia fights Germany in World War I.

1917 February revolution leads to abdication of czar and establishment of a provisional government.

1917 October revolution as Bolsheviks take control.

1918 Treaty of Brest-Litovsk with Germany takes Russia out of war.

1918–21 Civil war between "Red" Bolsheviks and "White" opponents.

1922 USSR set up.

1924 Lenin dies and is replaced by Stalin.

1941–45 World War II against Germany.

1953 Death of Stalin; Nikita Khrushchev takes power.

1957 USSR launches first space satellite.

1964 Khrushchev falls and is replaced by Leonid Brezhnev.

1985 Mikhail Gorbachev takes power and begins reforms.

1991 Boris Yeltsin is elected Russian president.

1991 USSR collapses as 15 new republics, including the Russian Federation, emerge as independent states.

1992 A new economic system is introduced to turn Russia from a communist into a capitalist state.

1993 A new constitution is introduced.

1994–96 First war against Chechen rebels.

1996 Yeltsin wins re-election as president.

1998 Economic collapse leads to devaluation of the rouble and severe inflation.

1999 Yeltsin resigns and hands over power to his prime minister, Vladimir Putin.

1999–2000 Second war against Chechen rebels.

2000 Putin wins presidential election.

2004 Putin wins re-election as president.

2008 Dmitry Medvedev is elected president, with Putin as prime minister.

2008 Russian troops intervene in Georgia.

2008 Constitutional amendments extend terms of president and Duma.

Glossary

abdicate To give up the throne voluntarily.

authoritarian Insisting on strict obedience to authority.

autocracy Government by an individual with unlimited authority.

autonomous Semi-independent.

Bolshevik Member of early Russian Communist Party.

censorship The banning or restricting of anti-government statements in the media.

communism Political system that believes in the common ownership of industry and property as controlled by the people.

constitution Written document setting out the principles by which a country is governed and the rights its people enjoy.

czar Title of the Russian emperors.

Duma The Russian parliament.

ethnic Relating to the common racial, religious and linguistic characteristics a group of people.

European Union Economic and political union of 27 European countries.

executive The branch of government responsible for carrying out the laws and running the administration of the country.

glasnost Policy of "openness."

KGB Komityet Gosudarstvjennoj Biezopasnosti, the Soviet secret service organization.

krais Territory of Russian Federation.

legislature The parliament or lawmaking branch of government.

market economy Economic system in which supply and demand, rather than state control, set prices and wages; also called a free market economy.

Muscovy Old name for the territory around Moscow.

NATO North Atlantic Treaty Organization, the defense organization founded in 1949 linking the US, Canada, and Western Europe, and now including many former communist states.

oblast Region of Russian Federation.

okrug Autonomous district in Russian Federation.

oligarch Person who exerts a strong influence on government or the economy and has great wealth.

perestroika Policy of "reconstruction."

Romanovs Ruling royal family of Russia from 1613 to 1917.

rouble Russia's currency, equal to 100 kopecs.

Rus The original inhabitants of Russia.

Siberia Asian territory of Russia.

Slav The main ethnic group in Russia.

steppes Grassy, fertile plains of southern Russia.

stock exchange Financial market in which shares or stocks in a business are bought and sold.

Tatars Mongol invaders of Russia.

tundra Vast, treeless region in the Arctic with permanently frozen subsoil.

Urals Mountain range that forms the boundary between Europe and Asia.

USSR Union of Soviet Socialist Republics, also known as the Soviet Union, the communist nation containing Russia and 14 other republics that collapsed in 1991.

usurper Person who seizes the throne illegally.

Warsaw Pact Military alliance of the USSR and Communist countries in Eastern Europe, formed in 1955 and disbanded in 1991.

Further information

Books

Adams, Simon. *Flashpoints: Russian Republics.* Franklin Watts, 2004.

Hingley, Ronald. *Russia: A Concise History,* rev. ed. Thames & Hudson, 1991.

Murrell, Kathleen Burton. *Eyewitness Russia.* Dorling Kindersley, 1998.

Websites

https://www.cia.gov/library/publications/the-world-factbook/geos/rs.html

CIA *World Factbook* entry on Russia:

http://russiatoday.com/Russia_Now/Basic_facts
Useful general information

Index

Page numbers in **bold** refer to illustrations and charts.